I0492544

How to start an online business in South Africa

The nuts and bolts of successful online commerce

JR Gertzen

Copyright © 2021 JR Gertzen

All rights reserved.

ISBN: 9798704600725

DEDICATION

For my wife Correen and children, Isla and Niamh

CONTENTS

1   Introduction   Pg 1

2   Nuts and bolts   Pg 7

3   Business Bank Account   Pg 8

4   Payment Processing   Pg 14

5   Setting your business up for success online Pg 22

6   Online Presence   Pg 28

7   Facebook   Pg 29

8   Instagram   Pg 35

9   Business website   Pg 39

10 Direct Communication Tools   Pg 43

11 Email Marketing   Pg 47

12 Shipping   Pg 51

13 In Closing   Pg 55

"It's the possibility of having a dream come true that makes life interesting."
— Paulo Coelho, The Alchemist

1 INTRODUCTION

"What is the world's greatest lie?" the little boy asks. The old man replies, "It's this: that at a certain point in our lives, we lose control of what's happening to us, and our lives become controlled by fate. But who knows? If we do our part, maybe the universe does so too?"
— Paulo Coelho, The Alchemist

Where it all started

"There is only one thing that makes a dream impossible to achieve: the fear of failure."
— Paulo Coelho, The Alchemist

In December 2019 I lost my job as an IT Operations Manager. It is not in my nature to sit around waiting for life to happen to me, so in January 2020 I started a food truck and catering business called Mo'Roccin, specialising in Moroccan food. I love cooking and have always had a fondness for the colours and flavours which Moroccan food brings to the table and wanted to share it with others. And most importantly, it would be a way to generate income.

I needed to be able to support my family financially.

One of the main obstacles I encountered with Mo'Roccin was that few people were familiar with Moroccan food, the second challenge was getting into markets to sell the food. The first few weeks were very hard; I didn't know how to engage with people, being from an IT background with the limited marketing and social skills normally associated with this discipline. So starting out, we made only a few Rands a day, and if I have to be brutally honest,

1

some days actually resulted in the business losing money. I wasn't able to support my wife and family the way I wanted to. Even my children's education became a daunting prospect when things started getting tough.

To make things worse, I felt terrible, because my wife was now the primary breadwinner and coming from a relatively conservative Christian background, this caused a lot of turmoil inside me. I was raised to be a leader for the family as well as a primary breadwinner but was now in the position where my wife had to take the responsibility for bringing home most of the bacon. It left me feeling like a failure, especially on days where we actually lost money at the food markets.

Then Covid19 hit and Mo'Roccin was mostly shut down, together with the majority of the hospitality industry in South Africa. As the levels lifted, I was finally able to at least make some money by doing food orders and delivering it to my customers, but the final nail in the coffin was the reopening of fast-food chains. It was just no longer sustainable to run Mo'Roccin and I had to shut it down for good.

Re-invent

"When we love, we always strive to become better than we are. When we strive to become better than we are, everything around us becomes better too."
— Paulo Coelho, The Alchemist

Refusing to accept defeat and continuing to apply for positions in my field of IT Operations, the idea came to me to turn my passion, something very close to my heart, into a business, and so Beyond Marksman was born – an online sporting goods company focusing on hunting, target shooting and marksmanship. Even with Covid19 restrictions in place, I could trade and show a profit using couriers to deliver goods to my clients. Things were starting to look up. In just the first few months of online marketing for Beyond Marksman, we started building and growing a community of interested patrons and clients, and advertised the products on Facebook. I made a good number of sales by employing a free Facebook advertising strategy. But as Lockdown was extended with negative consequences for the hospitality and tourism industry, and hunting season was all but cancelled in 2020, sales started to drop.

Beyond Marksman had once again hit a ceiling at the end of October. Our online followers were no longer growing and we battled to make sales. Not making sales meant that profits were decreasing more and more while expenses remained constant and Beyond Marksman started struggling to keep head above water.

For a second time that year, I found myself in a pit of despair. I was lying awake at night trying to come up with ideas to increase sales. I was worried about providing sufficiently for my family in terms of monthly expenses. I was failing fast. Mostly I was lying awake because it felt like I was completely failing my family. I had a lot of support from my wife and life partner, who tried her utmost to keep me positive, but at night… sleep wasn't coming, just like the money to cover all the expenses wasn't coming.

The problem was that, although I had a good online marketing strategy, I was just not reaching enough people. Compounding this, I found that most of the online tools and scripts available to grow e-commerce, were aimed at international markets, and therefore not immediately applicable to the South African market. This frustrated customers and business owners alike, and resulted in potential clients turning away and using more conservative avenues of doing business, i.e. patronizing brick-and-mortar stores. I was no longer able to grow and expand my customer base unless I could find a way to scale these hurdles. This was evident, every morning when I stared at my Facebook page likes and seeing the number was still stuck on 1176 followers, day after day. I became more and more depressed and worried as the days passed.

This very nearly meant the end of Beyond Marksman, and I hesitate to think what that would have meant for me, as well as my family. But one bright day in November, I noticed something which peaked my interest. One of my competitors somehow managed to run paid-for advertisements on social media. This was something I was unable to do up to that point, due to the nature of the products I was selling. Advertising merchandise related to target shooting and hunting, like silencers, bullets etc. was against Facebook community standards.

At once I realised, if my competitor was able to run paid-for advertising, and advertise successfully to the South African market, there had to be a way for me to accomplish the same. I started studying Facebook policies and community standards and I did a fair bit of research on Google to see how I can get around Facebook policies without breaking them. Breaking Facebook policies or community standards would end your business page in Facebook jail. I knew that if I landed up in Facebook jail, there would be hard consequences; I would have no way to market my products at all… for who knows how long.

Inspired by what I found, I did further research on how to market my products and not have Facebook reject my adverts. What I found not only gave me a way to place adverts and have them approved, but changed my entire life.

I learned that normal websites were no longer sufficient to sell products online, but that the way to effectively advertise and market my business and products were through social media and the use of a technique called sales funnels. And with a little applied IT skills, I could modify these as well as existing online marketing tools and e-commerce applications, so that they are tailor-made for the South African market.

Funnels will be discussed in detail in the sequel of this book, which deals with online marketing strategies. However, for the purpose of this background story, suffice it to say that it is a powerful marketing tool aimed at focusing the attention of a scientifically chosen target market on your website. If you already have a business online or sales funnels peak your interest, you are welcome to have a look at The One Funnel Away. Here you can sign up and it is a four-week online course that will teach you on how to compile offers and build sales funnels from start to end.

As for me, all of a sudden, my followers on my business page started increasing again and so did my sales. The first month I implemented my online marketing tools and e-commerce applications, my sales literally doubled. I started to make money again. Suddenly I was spending R1000 per fortnight on Facebook ads, and that R1000 spend would bring in R12k in profit as well as new followers on my Facebook business page.

The one thing I have realised during my journey up to this point, is that there are so many moving parts that make up the backbone of a successful online store, that it becomes a daunting prospect. With my friends (and/or their friends) wanting to start up online businesses, I realised that there was a lot of information on the internet dealing with the subject, but very few of these actually helped to put everything together for the South African environment. Most successful entrepreneurs have to research and digest all this information and somehow incorporate it all into their business. And then, after going through all that trouble, they still need to figure out how to make it work for their particular market, in a South African environment, dealing in Rands, not dollars, and using the Metric system, not the Imperial system.

With this realisation, knowing that I had figured out much of the solution, I couldn't just sit by and let "my fellow South Africans" fail because the knowledge of what they needed isn't compiled in one easily digestible source. The Covid Pandemic has caused so much loss of income for South Africans, but we are the future of this country and what we create today, will soon become the backbone of our economy. We will not go silently into the night, but instead, create businesses that stimulate the economy and as we grow, start employing people. Slowly we will combat unemployment, which will give our fellow citizens the dignity to rise up from the ashes during these uncertain times, and help build a better future and a better country for all.

So I put together a plan, to start empowering South African entrepreneurs to start their own ventures online through an online training course. My departure point was to create an in-person online education session to educate South African entrepreneurs to either start or take their businesses online. Very eager to share my knowledge with fellow entrepreneurs, I set up my first online in-person training course and invited a few friends, who were starting or have just started new online businesses. Let's teach people to fish so they never go hungry!

But there was a problem. The first session which should only have been 2 hours ended up running way over 3 hours. There was simply too much information I had to convey. So I decided to write books containing this crucial information instead. And yes, I could easily condense this book to a tick list of what you need to have in place, but that does not answer the "Why?". Knowing what you need to be successful is one thing, but the most value is gained from understanding why it is that you needed each product. If you know why you need and use a certain product, it is more beneficial and you can then properly leverage those products to generate more income.

Potential

And with that, I created this first book in the series, which will explain all the tools I found to work for a South African market, and why and how we are using them to make our business online more successful. This will let fellow entrepreneurs (whether you are IT skilled or not) benefit from my learnings. One of my favourite quotes is the following; "Some people learn from other people's mistakes, other people are the other people". So this book is a combination of the successful tools, the nuts and bolts, that make up a successful online store and that works!

The next book in this series, after all the "infrastructure" is in place, will focus on how to start marketing your business online. We will cover free ways to advertise and market products and grow your audience, before moving to paid advertising and expanding your market, locally as well as internationally.

I already mentioned that I come from a strong IT (Information Technology) background. In general, IT people are very misunderstood. People tend to think that professionals in the IT industry chose that particular discipline because they do not want to engage with people. In my life, I have found this to be mostly untrue. Yes, it might be true that IT nerds do not know how to engage with other people, but understand one thing, people in the IT industry (yes they love solving problems), is in IT because they want to help others. Having moved out of the IT field, the urge to help is still inside me, and with this first book, I am taking my first steps to helping my fellow South Africans.

So this journey has led me down a path I would never have believed I could find myself on. I went from stumbling in the dark to actually showing profits. But most importantly, I have grown to the point where I am now in the position to help others also realise their own true potential.

"A funny thing happened on the way to my potential"
—   Anonymous,   The   Arabian   Nights

2 NUTS AND BOLTS

Since February 2020, the Covid pandemic has had an enormous impact on business worldwide. In South Africa alone it has been one of the biggest reasons for loss of income. Traditional businesses are battling to stay afloat and in many instances are either forced to reduce staff or to shut their doors completely. There are many South Africans who went from having a steady income before Covid19, to not having any income at all. The rules of traditional commerce seem to have changed overnight and people are forced to look at new ways of doing business.

In the past few months, I have had many friends and acquaintances mentioning an interest in starting an online business themselves, or friends who would like to start a business. The most frequently asked question I find myself answering is, "Where should I begin?" or "Do you have any pointers on where I should start?"

I gave this substantial thought and decided to write down the nuts and bolts which I have found useful in creating and running an online store in South Africa. I spent months researching these building blocks for my own business and find them to be the cornerstone of such a new venture. It is a competitive new world out there, and therefore, in order to professionally exchange goods for money in the world of e-commerce, it is critical to put everything in place to make the transaction as efficient, smooth and successful as possible.

So lets see what I use and what I think needs to be in place:[1]

---

1   Links contained in this book has been shortened using "bitly" for typeability.

3 BUSINESS BANK ACCOUNT

Why is it important to have a business bank account?

When you start your business, it makes sense to run transactions through your personal bank account. As you grow, you'll need an account dedicated specifically to your business.

There is a school of thought that at some point you will reach a point where your business transactions are greater than your personal transactions and that would be the signal to open a business bank account. I, personally, do not subscribe to that. I personally feel that is a loser strategy. If that is your mindset, it is a Plan B mindset and you will fail. Taking the step to open a business account already puts your mind in a state of positivity and closes the door on Plan B. It sets you up for success because you have taken the first step to have a legitimate business and gears your mind to make decisions to make your business a success. With a Plan B strategy, you are already giving yourself an out, should the business fail. With that mentality, you are already not focussing to do everything to make your business work.

To know more about Plan B, visit the link that I have posted at the bottom of this page.

Don't fail yourself, your business, and give yourself an out. Here is why:

Too many transactions to keep track of.

Having a separate business account will make it easier for you to manage your business. It is easy to collect receipts in the account as well as pay for business expenses with business money. A week or two down the line when you do the business books you will no longer have to remember if a PNA expense was for business stationary or beginning of the school year expenses.

As this whole series deals with an online business, you will most likely have online credit card processing and that money needs to go somewhere. You will have customers making EFT payments and you will pay suppliers, couriers and other services from your account. But mostly, when you log in to your business bank account, you will be able to see immediately be able to see where your business' finances are at. No more grabbing a calculator or spreadsheet to try and determine what money belongs to the business and what money belongs to you. The account balance will be what the account balance is.

Improving the image of your business.

Although people indeed buy from people (in the end), it is important to have a professional business image.

Firstly, when you are registered with a supplier under your business name and all of a sudden you make a payment from Joe Soaps account, it makes it harder for the supplier to allocate the payment because they thought they were dealing with XYZ company, so who is Joe Soap? Secondly, some suppliers require that you provide them with bank statements to register as an agent for their products. You might not want them snooping through your personal bank account. When dealing with suppliers, not having a business bank account damages the credibility of your business as a legitimate business and makes you look like you are sort of in business or even worse, you started just a few weeks ago.

Thirdly, when a customer wants to pay by EFT, don't be surprised when they order goods from XYZ company and then back out of the deal, once you provide them with Joe Soaps bank details. Your business account tells your customers that you are legit and that you are here to stay. A little piece of mind goes a long way to establishing customer trust. As a new business, reputation and trust with your customers will either catapult your business forward or sink it faster than the titanic.

You want to build a company image that conveys, strength and builds confidence with customers and suppliers. You want them to click the "Buy Now" button with confidence, knowing that they will receive the goods or services they purchased.

Protecting your personal identity.

As we will be predominantly be trading via online sales channels, there is a lot of value in protecting your personal identity. You will be handling several transactions from people you have- as well as people you probably will never meet in person. You will be sending them your bank account details for online payments (invoices as well as EFT payments). This means you will be sending banking information to fraudsters, as well as customers, and you won't be able to tell which is which when you send it. This makes it easy for fraudsters to start mining your information for potential identity theft or committing fraudulent activities.

Having a business account could minimise the damage to a dedicated business account. It will also make it easier for fraud investigators, should a fraud investigation be launched.

A business account, along with company registration, can go a long way in protecting your personal identity, identity number and your personal finances from criminal elements that would pay a handsome sum to gain access to your entire financial life.

It helps to build a relationship with your bank.

Your bank account will become more important as your business grow. You might want to invest, save, pay taxes and want to keep everything neatly in your own accounts so that the money doesn't get absorbed. You also want to build a credit profile for future growth and finance applications that will enable future growth.

You will also want to have a business debit or credit card, which could be used to make payments; in person or online.

Accepting Debit and Credit card payments.

This might be the single biggest reason why you would want a business bank account. The entire world trades with credit and debit cards and therefore you want to accept them as well. Customers like choice and therefore you want to offer them what is convenient for them to pay you. Therefore, make sure you can accept card payments as well as EFTs . One of the biggest motivators to accept credit or debit card payments are that when the transaction gets cleared, it shows in your payment processor account and shortly after that, it hits your bank account.

With that said, you want your business name appearing on your customer's card or bank statement and not some random Joe Soap (which they can't remember who it was or what they purchased). If your customer can't remember what they paid for or who Joe Soaps is, they might log it with their credit card provider as a suspicious transaction or worse, fraudulent.

Simplify tax preparations.

When it is time to pay tax to the receiver, your accountant (or you if you do it yourself) will love you for it. Separating business and personal expenses can be... rather complicated. Having a business account clearly distinguishes your personal from your business transactions. It can sometimes even be beneficial;
1. Some business expenses are tax-deductible.
2. If an accountant is doing your taxes, it will be cheaper as they do not have to spend additional time sifting through transactions to allocate them correctly.

Both of these examples could potentially either score you time and money or cost you. In one you might be paying higher taxes as something that was tax-deductible does not get deducted and in two your accountant, probably, don't work for free. It's the age-old saying of time is money!

When you enter into a partnership or register as a company.

When entering into a partnership, at least one person/partner is normally responsible for the financial transactions of the business. For this, a business account is paramount, as this simply can't be done with your personal account (nor should you want to give someone access to your personal account in the first place!)

Similarly when you register a company for your business. Not only might others want to access your bank account (accountants, suppliers wanting bank statements, etc.), but there could also be legal ramifications for sharing account access and personal liability.

Companies are viewed as a separate legal entity from their owners and therefore, just like you have a bank account, so should the business. Any transactions that run through your personal account for the business will technically be a separate activity. This will in the end need to be accounted for at the end of the tax reporting period, for the business as well as for your personal tax returns.

Selling the business.

There are various reasons why businesses get sold but for now, we need to look at the implications associated with the potential sale of your business.

1. When selling a business, it should have a bank account associated with it. This will be transferred to the new owners with the business' financial record.
2. It is an undisputed record of the performance of the business to potential buyers. Anyone interested in buying your business would like to inspect the financial statements, and this is normally the starting point.
3. The sale of a business usually triggers an investigation process very similar to an audit. The more substantive documentation you can provide, the better. Surely you don't want prospective buyers snooping through your personal bank statements.
4. A business bank account enables you to release bank statements to a prospective buyer, without the concern of disclosing personal information.

In Summary.

A business bank account makes sense for a variety of reasons. It is simpler, safer and more efficient than using your own personal account.

Plan B:
You can view the video here: https://bit.ly/39NwCYZ

The account I use:

For my online business, I use a TymeBank bank account. It is essentially two accounts in one. You first by signing up for a personal account, after which it allows you to sign up for a business account. The signup process is super simple and easy and can be done online here: https://bit.ly/3cGgxpG.

Why I chose TymeBank:
1. It is an online digital bank and everything can be from my phone app (or computer).
2. 70% of the time, EFTs from other banks still clears on the same day

that they are made (without your customer having to pay for forced clearance).

3. No monthly banking fees.
4. A debit card that I can use in-person and online.
5. I can do bulk payments to suppliers (both TymeBank and non-Tymebank).
6. I can accept payments in the form of till point payments.
7. It allows for up to 10 Goal Saves, which I can use to manage my business expenses (up to 7% interest per year).
8. Daily limit of R200,000 for transacting (online purchases, card purchases, cash withdrawals, payments, cash sends, etc.).

Are all TymeBank transactions free?

Sadly not all transactions are free. As a small business owner (for now), this account makes more sense than having a business account at one of the long-established banks. Even though there are transactions that you do need to pay for, my online business only uses about 10% of them. When I tally up all those transaction costs, it ends up a fraction of the cost of your monthly account fees (just for having the account before trading) at one of the established banks.

To find out more about what TymeBank offers, visit their site https://www.tymebank.co.za.

4 PAYMENT PROCESSING

About payment processing.

When goods are sold, there is always an exchange of goods for money. This money can be exchanged in various forms. The oldest of this is of course cash. Cash is still very popular, despite the many other forms of payments, due to several reasons. Number one is possibly because no-one knows how much of it is stashed under your pillow. The problem with cash is, that for an online store, chances are good that you will never see the customer to make the exchange; goods for cash, and therefore accepting cash payments, this might pose a problem to your online business. For most of your online transactions, you will most like conclude your deal using a form of electronic payment. Electronic payments in itself has many forms ranging from credit or debit cards, EFTs, cryptocurrencies and many others. Let's delve into what they are and why you should accept them.

What are electronic payments and why you should accept them?

Electronic payments refer to any digital form of payment made with a debit or credit card as well as Electronic Fund Transfers (EFTs). We'll categorise payments into two categories for the purpose of this document; Online Payments (credit or debit cards) and EFTs.

There are a lot of reasons why you should accept online payments, the first and foremost being that you are an online store and 99% of the time, you will not be in a position to exchange goods for cash in person, but here are a few more good reasons:

1. Reach more customers. More and more consumers are shopping online.
2. Sell more. Your market is bigger and not bound to your physical location.
3. Enhanced security. Banks and card providers are tightening security and verification protocols, making it harder to create fraudulent transactions.
4. Increase productivity. With integrating some of the online payment methods into your online store, it can eliminate manual tasks like updating payments.

Let's have a look at electronic payments and see what is available to an online store.

EFTs.

EFT is the process of transferring money from one bank account (for example your customer's bank account) to another bank account (for example your business account) to pay for goods and services.

Benefits of accepting EFTs as payment:
- It is the most cost-effective way of doing business and virtually free.
- It is secure as no physical cash needs to be handled.
- Less administrative procedures.
- It is traceable should any customer queries arise.
- If your customer/supplier account is at the same bank, it is virtually instant.

Disadvantages of using EFTs as payment:
- If the customer/supplier account is at a different bank, it could take up to a day or two to reflect in the receipts account.
- If a customer is in a hurry, because of the above point, it could delay a sale.

But all is not lost. A customer that is "in-a-hurry", can still commence after an EFT has just been done, but it will involve manually contacting the customer's bank. This way you can check the validity of the transaction against the transaction identification number. To do this, simply phone the bank where the payment originates from (customer's bank) and provide them with the transaction id displayed on the proof of payment received. The consultant will easily be able to confirm if the transaction is valid and the sale can conclude.

Online Payments.

To process card transactions online, you will either require a Merchant Account or a Payment Gateway.

Merchant accounts.

A merchant account enables you to accept credit/debit card payments. Obtaining a merchant account from your bank could also provide you with a card machine which can be used in-store but most importantly allow you to accept online card payments. Merchant accounts can also be obtained from payment gateways and some will also be able to provide you with a physical card processing machine.

For now, let's look at the traditional bank-issued merchant account. This type of card processing account is directly connected to your bank account. Therefore it will show you the funds in your business transactional account as well as merchant account when you log into your business banking account.

Benefits of bank-issued merchant account:
- All your banking can be in one place.
- Normally get issued with a manual card machine for in-person processing.
- Costs - Pay a lower rate (at first) for processing card transactions.

Disadvantages of bank-issued merchant account:
- You might be required to have more than one bank account at different banks to cater for the eventuality that the merchant portal is off-line and can't process transactions at the time.
- Integration into your website might be a little harder and you might be required to get an external company to do the integration for you.
- Costs
  - You might need to make a minimum amount of sales to leverage from the better card processing fee.
  - If you fail to make a minimum amount of sales, you could potentially also have to pay a card machine rental fee for that month (or it goes higher for that month).
- TRUST – Your customers don't know you (yet) and therefore might not feel 100% safe giving you their credit card details. They are unsure as to how (or who did) the integration into your

website is done, where their card details will end up.

For me, trust mentioned in the disadvantages above is a huge thing and if you are just starting, know that it is huge. Still today I get customers wanting to order from my online shop, but they phone me to see if a real person picks up the phone, and only after talking to them (be knowledgeable about your products) do they complete their sale. Because of this, I lean heavily towards using a payment gateway as opposed to a straight forward merchant account.

Payment Gateways.

Payment gateways are almost magical things. For one, your payment gateway provider will issue you with a merchant account. Secondly, they are already known to your customer and have established trust. Thirdly, they are easy to integrate into your online store or website.

But what is a payment gateway and how do they work?

I can ramble for the next few pages on what exactly they are and how they work, but I'm rather going to explain it as simple as possible. A payment gateway collects the money from your customer and places it into your merchant account held with the payment gateway itself. After a set amount of time, the money is released into your business bank account.
Some payment gateways are quick in getting the money into your account, for example, Yoco, where you have your money the next day. Some payment gateways are a bit slower.

As mentioned above, your payment gateway has already established trust with your customer. Taking Yoco as an example again, your customer probably knows about or have swiped their card on a Yoco terminal already. Therefore if they see the Yoco logo on your website and know that Yoco will be processing the transaction, a certain level of trust with doing business with your business has already been established, by your payment gateway.

Payment gateways are great because they are easy to integrate with your shopping cart. Most of them already have out of the box plugin that integrates with your online shop, so you just have to click the install on the back-end of your online shop. That is like having your phone and having a Bluetooth speaker. With minimal effort, you pair your phone with your Bluetooth speaker and off you go. Integrating a payment gateway is usually just as simple.

Benefits of payment gateways.

- Easy checkout – makes the customer checkout experience easy as they most likely have followed the checkout process before.
- TRUST – They know their transaction and card details are handled by a company the trust.
- Impulse purchase – Once a checkout experience is too tedious or complex, they might abandon the sale. Payment gateways help to keep it easy and some even have a "Buy Now" button.
- Payment Gateways
  - ☐ Normally easily integrates with your shopping cart.
  - ☐ Provides fast payment processing.
  - ☐ Accepts multiple payment options.
  - ☐ Provides chargeback prevention.
  - ☐ Provide fraud management.
- Security – They are compliant with the security standards like 3D secure etc. for providing secure transactions.

Disadvantages of payment gateways.

- Payments may be held for a certain amount of time before it is released.
- If a fraudulent card is used to complete a transaction, the monies could potentially be reclaimed from your business (cost of doing business, unfortunately).
- The customer sees that there is an intermediary and that the payment is not going to you directly.

Cost of doing business – This is money your business spends without getting reimbursed. Like, to process a card transaction with your merchant account or payment gateway charges a minimal fee. You pay it and enjoy the benefits of being able to accept card payments. It might be a grudge purchase, but it provides benefit.

Payment gateways I use:

It is certainly easier just to manage one payment gateway, but I have found that providing options for the customer has a higher sales turnover as your customer is most likely to select the payment option he knows or trust. For my online store, I use the following payment gateways (yes, I use all of them).

Yoco:

Yoco can be used for in-person point of sale purchases. The customer can physically insert, swipe or tap their card at your store or stall. It can also be used to accept online payments, using a payment link or a payment request, which your customer can action using his/her card. Yoco is also very innovative and keeps adding ways to get paid to their stall of offerings.

Sign-up: https://bit.ly/39NCd1r
Sign-up is free and there are no monthly costs. Should you wish to have a point of sale terminal, these can be bought at sign-up or separately.

What Yoco provides:
- The higher your turnover, the lower your transaction fee becomes.
- You can send payment links to customers and never have to handle their card details.
- Free Yoco App for your phone.
- Free business portal for reports, performance and dashboards.
- Expert support and solutions 365 days a year.
- Accepts all major cards.
- *No monthly fees.*
- You receive your cash within 2 working days (usually faster).
- Yoco Developer help for integrations.
- Have native integrations to some of the leading online store software like WordPress, WooCommerce and a few other.

PayFast:

PayFast is predominantly an online payment gateway. It offers no point of sale terminals and I have found it easy to integrate. Because they have been around for a while, it provides more native integrations to a wider amount of online shops including Shopify.

Sign-up: https://www.payfast.co.za
Sign-up is free and there are no monthly costs.

What PayFast provides:
- Various payment methods including cards, instant EFTs, mobicred and more.
- Free sales dashboard for your sales.
- Have a profile per customer to make checkout easier and faster.

- Easy fee structure.
- Can send the customer a payment request.
- Merchant and buyer support.
- Accepts all major cards.
- *No monthly fees.*
- PayFast Developer help for integrations.
- Have native integrations to some of the leading online store software like Shopify, WordPress, WooCommerce and a few others (to the total of 80+ shopping carts).

Snapscan:

Snapscan is predominantly an in-person payment solution. By using your phone, you scan a barcode displayed by a merchant, and payment is completed on the customer's phone. It can also be used as an online payment option and full or partial integration can be done. It is convenient when a customer has forgotten his/her wallet.

Sign-up: https://www.snapscan.co.za/
Sign-up charges are minimal amount for shipping your first barcode and there are no monthly costs.

What Snapscan provides:
- You display a barcode and the customer scans and pays for it via his phone.
- Free sales dashboard for your sales.
- Dynamic fee structure, the more you sell the less you pay for card transactions.
- Merchant and buyer support.
- No monthly fees.
- Excellent customer support and willing to assist with integrations.
- Have native integrations to some of the leading online store software like Paygate, OpenCart, WooCommerce and a few others.

PayPal:

Although this is the one I use the least, it is still great to have it and offer it as a payment alternative. It is a worldwide trysted payment gateway and it offers almost integration into any online store you could probably imagine. As they say on the PayPal website, "Sell without boundaries". Withdrawing fund in South Africa could be a bit tedious and requires either an FNB bank account or using Xoom.

Sign-up: https://www.paypal.com
Sign-up is free and there are no monthly costs.

What PayPal provides:
- Global customer base.
- Transactions in a various amount of native currencies.
- Balance kept in USD (other currencies possible).
- Many people have PayPal accounts (even South Africans)
- Easy fee structure.
- Can send the customer a payment request.
- Can send and receive payments to suppliers, customers or friends.
- Merchant and buyer support.
- Accepts all major cards.
- No monthly fees.
- PayPal has excellent Developer help and documentation for integrations.
- Have native integrations to some to virtually all online shopping platforms and if not, a Google search will find you someone that has done it to your specific shopping cart.

Xoom (a PayPal service):

Xoom is a service provided by PayPal that allows you to make deposits into all major South African banks. It does charge a transaction fee per deposit into a South African bank, but its the easiest way to get your Dollars into a South African bank account. As with all foreign exchanges the Exchange rate they offer might be different from the actual exchange rate at the time.

Sign-up: https://www.xoom.com
Sign-up   is   free   and   there   are   no   monthly   costs.

5 SETTING YOUR BUSINESS UP FOR SUCCESS ONLINE

About building your brand.

Building a strong online presence and trust with your customers is of paramount importance. Next, we will focus on your brand. This includes the following elements:
1. Domain Registration for your business.
2. Email hosting and productivity tools.
3. Logos.

Domain registration.

Deciding on- and registering a domain name should not be done in haste. This will become part of your identity online. It is a valuable marketing and search tool which will lead customers to your website. It is one of the most important decisions you will make when carving out your slice of the online market.

The Internet has transformed the way small business owners gets things done. Whatever your business is doing online, it starts with your domain name. It identifies you, your brand, your business and attracts customers. It is also the first impression visitors get of your business.

Choosing a strong domain name brings with the following:
- It adds professional credibility to your business, separating you from millions of get-rich-quick websites on the internet.

- Provides visibility for your brand, much like a storefront window, a good domain name will create awareness and attract customers to your business.
- It establishes your online business as a tech-savvy and forward-thinking company. It is crucial to your reputation to claim your territory online!
- It creates mobility for your internet presence. If you decide to change web hosting services, relocate to a different country, your domain name stays with you and your business. This allows you to continue building your brand without having to start over.
- It increases your search engine listing ranking. As you build your business, your domain name will become more recognizable to search engines like google. This will lead to bringing more customers your direction.
- Domain names can pose your business on a world stage or create a focus in a specific region or country. In short, going dot com (.com) or going dot coza (.co.za).
- Domain names are a cheap value add to your business and have a low annual maintenance fee.

Choosing a domain name:

A new start-up business should always strive to select a domain name that parallels or even better, match the company name directly, as to avoid creating confusion. A domain should also be unique and available as a domain name before you announce it to the world. If you already own an existing business and your company name or certain keywords are not available, a little creativity might get you there.

Your domain name should be catchy and easy to remember. If at all possible, keep it short with the guideline of making it 6-10 characters long, with 8 characters being the sweet spot. The longer the name, the more opportunity of people misspelling it and never get to your site!

Simple, concise and typeable should be the rule over longer more descriptive names.

Having chosen a business name, especially for us living in South Africa, always try to get the coza and the dotcom. The reason I say this is because people can't always remember if the domain is a dotcom or coza.

Besides dot com and coza, many other domains could be used, which can be

very descriptive to your business, examples are:
- .restaurant
- .properties
- .club
- .tours

For example, your company might be doing tours in the Karoo and therefore you might register your company as **karoo.tours**. I would however suggest when doing this, also grab the coza or dotcom domain.

I use two registries to register my domains:

Mydomain.com – https://bit.ly/36F1jgW
I use this for all my dotcom and international registrations. Different top-level domains have different prices, but dotcoms retail normally for $9.99 (roughly R15.50).

domains.co.za - https://www.domains.co.za/
I use them for all my coza registrations. Registering a coza domain with them retails normally for R79. You can also use them for dotcom and a few other domains, but dot-coms are a bit more expensive with them. Plus, after your register the coza, we will end up configuring it so that we can manage the domain in mydomain.com.

Email hosting and productivity tools.

email@rockyour.domain

Many businesses use generic email addresses to conduct their business and that is ok. But as a start-up, you want to convey an image of professionalism, legitimacy and trust. Thus a proper email address should include your business' domain name. (i.e. @xyzcompany.com). By having a proper email address at your business name, you represent your company as a well-run, legitimate business.

You will also be emailing your customers from the business address. Mailing your customer from a generic email address xyzcom@gmail.com makes it harder for customers to find your business website. However, should you be mailing customers from joe@xyzcompany.com, the customer can just copy everything after the "@" sign, paste it into their URL and there is your website.

The fact that some business owners decide not to set up a domain email address is a missed marketing and branding opportunity. Having all the branding power of a business domain name and then using gmail.com, is a big mistake you should avoid.

Having an email address at your companies domain is the foundation to establish credibility. The most common expectation these days are that a company will have the following; a business name, some level of branding (company logo and some marketing materials or business cards), a website and a Facebook page.

Productivity tools

As a business, you need some productivity tools. As we are mostly focussing on an online store, your productivity tools need to be mobile as well. Something that will work on your laptop as well as your phone so that information is always within reach.
The most important of these productivity tools are usually; email client, document storage, a calendar, a document writer, a spreadsheet and some way to put a presentation together.

I found the easiest to accomplish all this is to use Google Workspace (formerly known as G-suite). Not only does it allow you to create documents, spreadsheets, presentations forms and much more, it is also a collaboration suite. You can easily share documents with customers or team members. You get to decide who has got what access (can they only read or are they able to update the documents as well). It also tracks changes and a history of versions, so it is easy to see who changed the document and what that person did to the document. But best of all, it saves documents automatically, should you lose power for whatever reason, your creation is safe.

For a minimal amount ($4.80/user at the time of writing) you can get all this and more. The best is, **you can also connect your business domain to your business mail address.**

Gmail is a powerful mail tool and as a business; having your email address on your Facebook page, possibly your website and other places (sending customers emails), you will likely receive more spam as time progress. One thing Google is very good at is SPAM filtering, so for this reason alone, it is a wise idea to host your mail with Google.

To sign up for Google Workspace, you can visit the following link: https://workspace.google.com

Logos

Whenever one talks about a well-established brand like Nike for instance, one immediately forms an image in your mind of the logo. Logos are part of your brand and go hand in hand with your domain. It will be placed on your Facebook business page, your website, at the bottom of your email and promotional materials like flyers, business cards, advertisements. Whenever someone says your business name or mentions your domain name, you want people to have an image of your business. That image starts with a logo.

Here are some reasons as to why your business should have a logo:
- It grabs customers attention.
- It makes a strong professional first impression.
- It's one of the foundations of your brand identity.
- It's memorable (see Nike example above).
- It separates you from your competition
- It fosters brand loyalty.
- But most importantly, your audience expects it.

There are several ways to go about logo creation.

The first, very expensive one (or free if you have a friend that's a graphic designer) is to have it created by a professional graphic design company. The graphic design company you approach will consult with you, find out about your business and then have their designers come up with a few brand identities or logos for you to choose from. If you have the money to spare, it will most likely be worth the cost. You will end up with a product that is much closer to the picture you have in your mind of your business and will most likely be very unique.

The second is to post a job on a freelancing website, like fiverr.com or freelancer.com (or many others), where you could get the same (or at least close to) as getting a professional company to do it, but at a fraction of the cost.

Lastly, you can use an online web tool to create your first logo. It has a few generic questions that you complete and puts together a logo for you using templates and scripts built into the logo creator website. The reason I say the first logo, is that you might get to a point where you want to re-brand. You might feel you have outgrown your old logo, or you have raised enough money to approach a professional. I have never rebranded, so I would tread when considering re-branding at a later stage. Up to now, we have spoken a lot about brand identity, trust and building a credible business reputation. So if you choose to use a free logo creator, keep on regenerating the logo until you have something that you really like or speaks to you about your business. Don't just take the first logo that pops up.

I usually turn to Hatchful, provided by Shopify. You can check it out here: https://hatchful.shopify.com/

Hatchful boasts 140,000+ business owners using it, of which I am one. One of the great things about Hatchful is that it not only creates you a logo, it creates you an identity pack. The pack not only includes your logo, but it also includes social media banners, profile images and headers that you can just upload to your website or social media pages (Facebook business page, Twitter account, YouTube account and much more).

6 ONLINE PRESENCE

This whole series is around starting up a business and in particular an online business. So far we have discussed; Business Bank Accounts, Payment Gateways and Corporate Image or branding. These are the cornerstones of your business, as businesses are primarily created to make money, and the first part of the series deals with where to put your money and how to get paid, as easily as possible. Lastly, it deals with what is the picture or image, a customer forms in his mind, when he thinks about your business or brand.

Next, we have to put the tools in place for your online presence. If you had a brick and mortar store, you would have a storefront that is inviting to customers. Next, we have to talk about your storefront or display window online. I primarily use three mediums to pose a storefront to customers. Whichever one you decide to utilise is up to you. If you ask me, use all of them. There are some other tools and mediums you can use outside of what I discuss, but I have not yet engaged with them and therefore they are beyond the scope of what we are creating here.

7 FACEBOOK

So what is Facebook?

"Facebook is a website which allows users, who sign-up for free profiles, to connect with friends, work colleagues or people they don't know, online. It allows users to share pictures, music, videos, and articles, as well as their thoughts and opinions with however many people they like." - from https://www.webwise.ie/parents/explained-what-is-facebook-2/

Facebook sounds super cool and it's free, or is it? If you don't pay for a product or service, it means you are the product. It is no different with Facebook. Facebook's power lies in its ability to form a profile of its users, which uses it as a connection tool with their friends, coworkers and people they have things in common with (interest groups) and sells advertising to businesses. This allows your business to effectively target Facebook users with its products.

If you were to utilise your ad spend to put up a huge billboard, a lot of what you pay for goes into displaying your product to everyone who sees it. Yes, people who might be interested in your product or service might see it, but a lot of what you pay for is seen by people who might not be interested. This is what makes Facebook powerful. Because Facebook forms a profile of each of its users, you can laser-target a segment of people who would be most interested in your product or service. Therefore, you spend money on the people who are most likely to buy your product or service.

So Facebook's user base gets access to the platform for free, but businesses pay to use it as a powerful promotional tool. So let's discuss in more detail why you should have a Facebook page for your business.

Learn about your target audience.

Facebook creates focus groups for you automatically and you can therefore directly communicate with your target audience. On Facebook, fans of your page are fans because they are aware of you and they like, want or need your product or services. They like your page because they are genuinely interested in you, your product or service. It also provides you with powerful Insights which lets you collect useful information about your audience. Their likes and dislikes, their age, their gender and what medium they predominantly use to interact with you. Facebook Insights also gives you a view of how your fans interact with you and how much they Like or Love your content or products and it also allows them to interact directly with you with comments on your posts. Use this power wisely. It is so easy to mute a comment, but it is more powerful to show your audience how well you can correct a problem or issue that might arise with your product or service and build trust and a good relationship with your audience.

Another thing that makes Facebook great is that it helps you to build your community. With Facebook algorithms, it will also display a post on your business page to friends of people who like your page, because if person A likes it and he is friends with person B, chances are that person B might also like your product or service.

It humanizes your company.

Facebook is all about community and social connections. Building a community and using genuine communications are integral parts of social media. It allows you to attach a face, name and a personality to your business. It gives you a chance to interact with your customer on a one-on-one basis. Use this power to connect with your fans with business and non-business interactions. Business; "we are launching this new product", or non-business, yes sometimes post a joke or something lighthearted (but keep it professional - profanity is not your friend). Make your company human and show your audience that it is a business that cares.

Does this mean you have to sit for hours a day doing this? The answer is "No", but put aside an hour a day to react, comment, reply and like posts and comments of your fans. For the rest, Facebook has powerful scheduling tools, which allows you to automate a lot of your presence online, to give the feeling that you are there, even if you are in a meeting with a supplier or customer.

You can automate a lot and still give your fans a richer human relationship that goes beyond normal customer service.

Build a Community.

I have already referred numerous times to community fans and the like. The people who like your page are part of your business' community. Use this to get reviews of your products and get feedback. If your post is interesting and profound, you will most likely get a lot of interaction from your community. You can also use this to see what works and what does not. When you have a post with 100 likes, look at it. See why it worked and what triggered people to interact with it. If it gets little or no likes, look at it as well and analyse how it can be changed or improved to get more likes or if it seems like it got disapproval from your audience or fans, stop posting that particular type of post.

Search engine optimization.

Facebook is very useful for directing traffic to your website. Facebook posts and links also get indexed by search engines. Having rich content can boost your search engine rankings. The higher you rank on Google, the more trust there is in your business and ultimately your product or service. It's like when you search for a product or service on Google, you might page down to page 6, but if you didn't find what you are looking for in the first few pages, you are most likely to change your search criteria, rather than paging through pages upon pages of search results. Google will rank your page based on relevance to what the user searched, so utilise Facebook and use rich content to get your website, if not number 1, at least in the first 3 pages of a Google search result.

Your competition has one.

Customers like to search for products and services they need. They do it in Google and they do it on Facebook. Facebook will almost always be a port of call as not only does it allow customers to see what other people wrote about- or feel about you, but it also gives customers a feel for you and your business. Remember, if they can't find you or your products on Facebook, they will find your competition.

Allows you to get in front of your customers every day.
Regular updates, shares, links and videos give you a daily change to interact with your customers. With over 2.4 billion people on Facebook, there are a lot of problems your business can solve or provide a product that will solve their

problem. Make sure daily that your customers or fans know about you, your business and the products and services you can offer to solve their problems...

Free marketing.

Your Facebook business page is a place where you can market your products or services for free. This comes back to building your community. If you have 10 followers and you post an article or product, you will have 10 potential customers that will see it. If you build your fans to 10,000, one post will potentially reach 10,000 people that likes and follows your page and the best is, they are there because as previously stated, they care about your business, products or services already. So you post are already reaching the people that want to support you or purchase your products or services.

So make sure you start building your audience/fans/followers today because when you post to your page, you are already "preaching to the choir". You are offering products and services to people and customers that are already likely to buy from you.

Paid marketing.

NILIF - Nothing in life is free. Unfortunately, you will have to at some point start promoting your products and services using paid-for ads on Facebook. Make sure your business page and ad account are correctly set up. Every time you boost a post (paid advertising) or create a paid ad on your business page, it will show it to potential customers. Don't begrudge this. It is a wonderful way to firstly pose your products or services to new customers and secondly, it shows that the paid-for ad is sponsored by your business.

Why is this important you might ask? Well, customers can either click on your ad or post which will direct them to your chosen location, a WhatsApp contact, a post on your business page (where they can like your page and your other posts) or they can click on your business name in the "Sponsored by <Your Company Here>" section. Clicking your business name in the sponsored by section of the ad will redirect them to your business page. If they like what they see, they will like your page. This will grow your audience or fans and when your audience grows, even before boosting a post, your fans will get your new posts and it gets displayed to them, getting back to free marketing.

As set out in the beginning, with the billboard example, you want to maximise your ad spent. Facebook is phenomenal at this because it knows your customers, their likes, sex, age and online habits (and a lot more). This allows you to target the ads you create to people and potential customers that are most likely to interact or purchase your products and services. So your advertising spent is maximised as your ad will hit potential customers that are most likely to interact or buy products and services from your business.

Brand Loyalty.

As long as you provide valuable or entertaining content, your followers will come back for more and stay loyal to your brand and business.

Reach people on their phones.

Facebook is optimised for computers, phones and tablets. This allows you to reach your customers professionally, as Facebook does all the heavy lifting for you in presenting your content to its user base. It comes back to, don't make it hard for customers, who are the people you want to give you money, to find you.

Spy on your competitors.

This topic alone probably warrants a few extra pages or even a book, but I'll try to keep it sweet and short. Facebook not only allows you to Facebook stalk people but also your competitors. You can easily see or get a feel for what they are up to. From my personal experience, when I post an ad or new product or service, it is not long before my competitors follow suit. Know this, your competitors are spying on you, so return some professional courtesy and do the same to them. Follow their pages to see what they post and even visit their pages.

Visiting competitors' business pages can give you powerful insight into what they are doing. Recently Facebook even added a feature that allows you to see what "Paid for Ads" your competitors are running. Facebook also allows you to add your competitors to "Pages to watch". This is a great feature under Insights that allows you to benchmark your Facebook business page against competitor pages and see how you are doing.

Online shopping.

Facebook also allows you to run an online shop directly from your Facebook page. This allows you to sell directly through Facebook. A great thing is, that you can tag your products in your Facebook store in photos and posts, to make it easier for people to find them and purchase them.

Signing up for Facebook:

Sign-up: https://www.facebook.com/
Sign-up is free and there are no monthly costs. Creating a Business Page for your business is also free.

8 INSTAGRAM

So what is Instagram?

"At its most basic, Instagram is a social networking app which allows its users to share pictures and videos with their friends. The app can be downloaded for free from the usual app stores and takes pride of place on many a young person's (and older!) smartphone." - from https://www.webwise.ie/parents/explained-image-sharing-app-instagram/

Once again a "free" product that you can use to market your business. This should sound familiar if you read the piece about Facebook. Instagram is a platform that allows you to share videos and photos to friends, family and followers. It also allows you to share your business live and in real-time with your customers. If something happens, like your cat eating your laptop cable and you can't fill a customer order… Well, show your audience your human side and post it to Instagram via your phone. Or, if you have a product that you just received and will make available via your online store, share it.

And why would we do this? We want to humanize our businesses. We want to connect with our customers on a personal level. We want to show them that they can trust us because we really have what we say we are selling, or just connect with them by showing that life happens to us as well. There is a reason that so many people watched Big Brother. So let's discuss in more detail why you should have an Instagram for your business.

More people are using it.

Instagram has over a billion users and is growing. At least half of these users are active daily on the platform. It is primarily a photo or short 15-second video, which can be easily consumed by the Instagram user. A photo says a 1000 words, and that is the magic of Instagram. Quick bite-size chunks of information presented using either photos or videos.

Any size business can thrive.

Instagram is being used very successfully by very big corporates and small businesses alike. You can be a small business and still have a large Instagram following. It is very useful to get your business on the map and to start traffic to your main website. To successfully raise brand awareness, you should focus on creating an active presence. This involves posting at least 1 post per day.

You can make money directly through Instagram.

Instagram features a shop tab where customers can directly discover and purchase products from your store. A clever way of using Instagram is by creating a shoppable post. This consists of a cleverly constructed photo with product placement. The product gets tagged in the photo and links back to a product in the shop where customers can then purchase it. This is even more successful using influencers.

Partner with influencers.

Influencers are online celebrities that often promote a brand or product and take it mainstream. Influencers normally have thousands of followers (some have millions). Partnering with a dependable influencer can bring your company sales to a new level as well as hit demographics you might not normally be able to reach. A well-known influencer can publicize your company to millions of followers with just a few short posts, photos and product placements.

Stories make your business more relatable.

Instead of being just a faceless corporation, use Instagram to show customers your company's human side and make your company stand out from the crowd. Use live posts and stories to give your customers a behind-the-scenes look. Why should you do live posts?

Live posts are an excellent way to build a rapport with your customers. It creates trust and credibility with your customers. It makes you more relatable as well as shows your audience that you are for real.

Hashtags can increase visibility.

Hashtags can separate your business from the crowd and clever use of it will make your business more visible. When Instagram users search for a specific hashtag, your post will appear in the search results whether they are following you or not. Instagram users can also choose to follow hashtags, which will include your posts even if they are not following you... yet. It is a great way to build your community online and motivate people to follow your brand.

Effectively engaging with your followers and customers.

People like to be heard and they like their opinion to be known. Social media platforms have become one of the biggest platforms where people can influence others and give their opinions. Even just liking your posts is a way for a person to express his opinion about your product or service. Instagrammers, therefore, enjoy liking, commenting and sharing posts they enjoy to express their opinion and get to be heard by others. The more likes one of your posts gets, the more likes it will get as more users will see it. If more users see it, more people will have the opportunity to like it, and the more the post gets liked, the more visible your company or brand becomes, which will also lead to more followers, which next time round will make you reach a bigger wider audience.

Mobility is KING.

From day one, Instagram was created to be an App on a phone. So any content you post to Instagram will display correctly on your customers' phone, just as you have designed it to look.

Looking at my website analytics, it shows that 90% of traffic to my website is from smartphones. Computers are seldomly used. More and more smartphone users are switching to Instagram on their phones as it has a cleaner style look over Facebook. Engagement on Instagram is also 10x higher, so you can't afford not to be on Instagram.

Your competitors have one.

Chances are, your competitors already have an Instagram account and they are utilising it to build their community and drive traffic to their websites. Make sure your products, services and brand also pop up when Instagram users do their hashtag searches. It also builds trust and relatability with your customers and poses you as a tech-savvy company.

Spy on your competitors.

Same as with Facebook, Instagram is an excellent tool to see what your competitors are up to. Make sure you know what they post and how often they post. Also, observe how they interact with their followers. Learn from what they do, if they do something right, learn from that but also if they do something wrong, learn from that as well.

Instagram offers many ways to be creative.

Instagram is a platform of many possibilities. Mix it up with competitions, shoutouts to your followers or suppliers. Use vivid images and videos to create engaging content. Use it to draw in your customers and grow your following and audience.

Reach new customers through advertising.

As with all the free methods to market your business, Instagram also offers you the opportunity to make use of paid advertising. Similar to Facebook, it allows for customizable and trackable advertisements. It allows you VERY specific targeting for the ads you post (as said before, spend your money rather on a potential customer than the hordes).

Just like Facebook, it collects valuable user data that you can use with your online marketing campaigns and give you insights about your followers. This information can again assist you in fine-tuning your marketing campaigns for higher conversion rates.

Signing up for Instagram:

Sign-up: https://www.instagram.com/

Sign-up is free and there are no monthly costs.

9 BUSINESS WEBSITE

What is a business website?

A business website is a space on the internet, just like a physical shop on a street, where you are fully in control. If you had a brick and mortar store, you would be able to choose the carpets (or tiles), the furniture, how products are displayed etc. Your website is the same, just in a digital format. Up to now, we have dealt with social media platforms like Facebook and Instagram, where you get to create and post content, but once you posted it, it's in the hands of the community (which will make or break you). This is different from your website. Here you have full control over how your products and information is represented.

These days 30-40% of small businesses are slow to get online. There are several reasons (mostly misconceptions) as to why this is. Websites are seen to be expensive, hard to maintain and update. Some feel they don't have the necessary skills to run a website.

Then there is the last group of people which feels that they have Facebook, Instagram or maybe other social platforms and that a website is so "the year 2000". So let's delve into why you should have a website, even if your business is running in the years after 2020.

Customers expect a business to have one.

If you write a book and publish it or even get it to be published by a large publishing house and people do not find your book on Amazon, the sad reality is that it's not a real book. If you do get published, your publishing house will most likely list it on Amazon, because they know if it is not there it is not a real book. The same holds true for your business website. People expect your business to have a website and if you don't have a website, people will think you are not a real business.

Customers like to research online before making a purchase and when they do their research, make sure they find your website. Furthermore, as discussed in the Instagram section, users are a lot more on their phones these days. People like tech-savvy companies because they see themselves as tech-savvy. If you don't have a website, it appears that your company is still stuck in the dark ages.

You control the information and branding.

I have already touched on this, but this is very important. When you have a website, you are in control of how your products and services are portrayed. You have the final say about your company, your products and services. Comments and reviews on Facebook are really great, but it should not be left up to a community to have the final say over your business and how it is presented to the public.

An official presence on the internet (your website) is like having a home. It's a place (on the internet) where you stake your claim and have a "physical" presence.

Most importantly, because it is your personal place, just like your house, you are in control of exactly what it looks like. You get to choose what it looks like and give your customers that connection to you, by showing them (by using your website) exactly who they are doing business with.

Makes you look reputable and trustworthy.

People will judge your credibility, based on your website. So when you do it, do it well. Ensure that there are no spelling mistakes and once you find them, update those pages without delay. We are all aware of the emails that go something like this: "Mister X from the etterneys ofice of the lait Mrs. Johanson. I am contacting you to infom you that she has left you a substancial amount of moni."

As part of staking your claim of the internet, it is also a very good idea to have a custom domain as already discussed. It makes you look professional. If you are currently hosting your website on a free platform, there is nothing wrong with it, but link it to your domain as already discussed. People can't remember: https://user.myfreehosting.online/~john/TheSnakePit and should they be able to remember it, they most likely might have a spelling mistake.

Having a website is like having a brick and mortar store with a door and a sign that says: "We are open! Come in".

You can sell products online and in person.

Having a website as- or with an online store allows you to not only sell products directly from your website but also in person. People like to Google to research products, or to find a specific product as close to them as possible. When people Google for products and services, Google normally starts by presenting them with businesses close to their current geographic location. Personally, I use the search term "<service/product> near me" quite often. Make sure your business and website show up when people are in your area and searching for products and services.

Your competitors have one.

Your competitors most likely have one already and if they don't, great news for you. This will make it easier for you to get your products and services on the first results page of Google. But once again, portray your business as a tech-savvy business and use this to differentiate you from your competitors. Make sure that when customers search for products and services, they find you, because if they don't. They find your competition.

Websites are affordable.

The first myth gets busted. Websites are expensive, no they are not. This used to be true back in the '90s, when hosting space and bandwidth, especially in South Africa, were quite expensive. These days you can have a professionally themed website at a very affordable price. There are even companies that allow you to have a basic account for free and you only start paying once you exceed certain thresholds for space (disk space) used or data (on their internet lines) used.

It is cheaper to have a website than paying a landlord for a brick and mortar store. You can run it from the comfort of your own home without having to leave the house. Websites, for the minimal monthly fee, also tend to reach more people on laptops and phones than a brick and mortar store through normal channels of advertising (print, billboards, your storefront).

Websites are easy to maintain.

Second myth gets busted. These days, even the biggest companies run their websites on Content Management Systems (CMS). A CMS is a software that resides on your hosting space which provides your customers with a frontend (your storefront so to speak) and you as the owner or administrator of the website, a powerful backend. Logging into the backend allows you to change the design (look and feel) of your website live and in real-time. It allows you to update content, whether it is text or feature-rich photos or videos, in real-time. With a CMS you can even log in to your backend and update content on the fly from your phone.

Most hosting providers will even include a CMS as part of your hosting and have sometimes several to choose from, like Joomla or WordPress and a few others. Having a professional website and having the ability to update it easily, is no longer just for the biggest companies who can afford to appoint a webmaster.

Customers near you.

I have already touched on this, but a lot of people these days do location-based searches. They might want to buy a dog toy, so they will open Google search and type something like "dog chew toys near me". This will have Google present them with companies that list the said product from closest to their current location to companies further away. When your customers are on their phone and on the go, having a website will ensure they find you.

Signing up for a website:

Because this series deals with an online store, the link is for Shopify.
Sign-up: https://www.shopify.com/
Sign-up is free for a 14-day trial. Thereafter $29/month for Shopify (3rd party integrations[2] are charged separately).

---

2   A note on 3rd party integrations. When you integrate a payment gateway, that natively plugs into Shopify for processing and clearing of credit card transactions, for example PayFast, with a Shopify integration, charge a small transaction fee which is added to your monthly billing.

10 DIRECT COMMUNICATION TOOLS

What are messaging apps (applications)?

Messenger apps allow users to communicate via text or voice notes. Communications can also be enriched using videos, photos, locations, documents etc. Most messengers, like WhatsApp, Signal, Telegram etc. offers end-to-end encryption between communicating parties, making it very secure.

Many customers have messaging apps which they use to keep in touch with friends and family. These days even grandparents use it to communicate with younger generations. The nice thing about messages, even if you are in a hurry, you can quickly pop a message to someone and read their reply later when you have time.

Messaging capabilities is unfortunately a part of doing business these days. Customers don't want to phone into a call centre and wait to speak to a human anymore (although you get some that still do). They would rather send a message on their chosen and trusted messaging app and expect your business to respond, whether its a product query, shipping query or sending you a proof of payment.

Online shops, as the name suggests, are also online 24/7 so customers will expect you to be as well... sadly. Don't be surprised if a customer messages you 10:17 p.m. on a Sunday night. However, most South Africans know that when they send that late Sunday night text, that you might only respond the following day. With that said, messages during core business hours (07:00-18:00) should be attended to quickly and efficiently. There is a bit of leeway with texts from 18:00-21:00 meaning that it's fine responding only after dinner or putting the kids to bed. Usually, after 22:00 I don't open the message and let it stand over to the next day, as you don't want to get into a 2-hour messaging conversation after 22:00.

So let's look at messenger apps in detail.

Private and secure.

As already said, most messaging apps provide end-to-end encryption between parties. This means that there can be no middleman that can intercept messages or snoop on your messaging conversion (unless they have access to your physical phone while it's in an unlocked state). Business' are required to verify their account on some platforms (like WhatsApp) which creates trust as the customer knows it is dealing with a verified business.

Be Accessible.

Customers are shopping all hours, day and night. Therefore, they request information all hours of the day. Messaging also fits some customers' personalities better and it allows them to interact with your business easier if they do not have to physically speak. It allows customers to contact you from their comfort zone. Not only is messaging quick and efficient, but it is also very reliable. A customer can communicate with you even they have bad cellphone reception. And if their message doesn't go through right away, they know that it will be delivered as soon as the communication is restored (whether their/your bad signal or a dead phone gets switched back on).

For your business, it allows you to respond directly to customers queries in a timely manner.

Understanding your customers.

Messaging allows you to interact directly with your customers one-on-one. You can utilise this to gauge customer preferences. You can also understand your customers better by sending them a quick poll or survey to complete. You can ask them questions.

It allows you "personal" contact with your customers and gives you a way to respond in a personal manner (humanize your business). The personal touch also conveys to your customers that you value them and their time.

Strengthen brand presence and credibility.

Communications between you and your customer are more personal and authentic. It opens the door for you to follow up with them regarding orders they received and how they find products and services that were offered. Getting a feel for your customer and knowing their likes and dislikes also allows you to present them with personalised promotions.

Quicker response times.

Messaging does help with faster customer service. It also allows you to assist multiple customers at the same time. 56% of people would rather use a messenger app to contact you/your business than phoning through a call centre. Messenger apps are also becoming more feature-rich and even allows you to create templates for messaging. This, in turn, can be used to for faster replies, like when a customer asks your bank account details for an EFT, instead of having to type it out, you can simply type the shortcut code example: "/banking") and the messenger app will complete the reply for you (give your banking details). Utilising the templates from the messenger app, you can easily build a powerful frequently asked questions library.

Using a telephone you can only respond to one query at a time. Using messaging, it is easy to communicate and respond with 2 or more customers at the same time.

Reach across generations.

Just like payment gateways, customers are more likely to interact with brands or businesses using a preferred messaging platform. Almost everyone with a cellphone uses a messaging app these days, from children to grandparents. No matter what age group your customer is, he/she probably has messaging in one form or another.

Future proof communications.

Some messenger apps allow you to label your contacts, which makes it easier to distinguish if a contact is a business customer or not, which allows you to prioritize your responses to more than one unread messages.

Communicate creatively.

As already said, some messenger apps allow you response templates, but not only does it have to be text, it can also include pictures, videos etc. as part of the template response. It allows you to send information on a product immediately, whether it be a pamphlet, foto or a video. You can even use voice notes for that personal human touch.

Customers expect every online business to respond in a timely manner. Usually, the quicker you are responding, the less likely it will be that they will take their business somewhere else. So love it or hate it, use messaging apps to communicate with your customers.

Messenger apps that I use:

Facebook Messenger

Sign-up: https://www.messenger.com/
Sign-up is free

WhatsApp Business

Sign-up: https://www.whatsapp.com/business/
Sign-up is free

Signal

Sign-up: https://signal.org/en/
Sign-up is free

Telegram

Sign-up: https://telegram.org/
Sign-up is free

11 EMAIL MARKETING

What is email marketing/list tools?

Communications with customers are not reserved for messaging apps. Email marketing is still very relevant, even today, to communicate with your customers. For one, it is customers that probably already purchased from you before or they already have an interest in your business and is on the list because they are likely to buy from you. So from this perspective, it is a no-brainer to use this virtually free marketing tool.

But do you have to type out thousands of emails? Luckily, not. Mailing list software like MailChimp gives you the ability to manage mailing lists, newsletters, automated campaigns and so much more.

Post-2020, why email marketing?

Although many people receive many forms of spam, remember, that most of those emails they received they signed up for. The ones that they find unuseful, they will unsubscribe from. The ones they do not unsubscribe from, usually are the ones they still look at. People will only unsubscribe from your mailing list if they feel your mails are not adding value to them.

With mailing lists, it is easy to build an international audience. The one thing that remains true is that when done right, mailing lists will catapult your business forward. When done wrong or not at all, will let you miss out on great opportunities. There is a simple formula or benchmark, once your mailing list is established to let you know you are doing it right. In general, you should make around R15 for every person on your mailing list per month.

So if you have 100 people, you should make R1,500. If your mailing list is 10,000 people, it should equate to R150,000

Ease of design & launching email campaigns.

You do not have to be a web designer these days to create beautiful and professional-looking email campaigns or emails. Software, for example, MailChimp, is completely template driven. You can add sections and shape your mail to look however you choose. You can change colours add headings, add photos, add videos.

To get your mailing list into the software, is very easy can be done manually (ouch) or via a contact list import (yay!). You can even tag groups of people in your mailing list for different campaigns or groups. Customers can also update their settings or profile information to enrich their experience. This again can be used to engage with your customer more targeted. An example would be, sending them a "Happy Birthday" email with an offer specifically tailored for them. Another would be, making an offer to everyone that resides for instance in a specific province.

The one biggest thing about using mailing list software is that they are built to play by the rules. If you try to send a mail to 1000 people using your email, chances are you will get blacklisted. Mailing list software is configured to release mails within a reasonable time to your audience which will avoid your address being blacklisted or listed as a spammer on spam filters.

Automated email campaigns.

Mailing list software is a great way to create automated campaigns that keep prompting a customer about your products. Once you add a customer or the customer adds him- or herself, it will initiate the campaign. The campaign can be set to send a series of emails. On day 1, it will send the customer product A & B for instance. On Day 2 it sends product C & D and so on. This will keep you in the front of their mind. A simple example of this is the simple signup form. Once the sign-up, it will send them a Welcome Email. Next level, is to create a campaign that will congratulate a customer on his or her birthday. This gives you a personal connection with your customer as they will feel your company cares and thinks about them on their birthday. But most importantly, you can keep in touch and send them your products or promotional offers.

Build your emails or campaigns online.

Mailing list software normally has a very easy to use interface with drag and drop functionality. It lets you create visually stunning emails that will grab customers attention. It allows you to add text, headlines, videos, images, links and much more.

It normally has an online viewer which will show you what the final product looks like and also allows you to test all your links in your mail to ensure that they are working properly. You do not want to send a mail with a broken link to a website or product. It also allows you to do inbox testing. This will give you a preview in your own mail of what your email or campaign will look like. Some software also has an inbox tester that will show you how the mail will be display in your customers' inbox with over 40 different clients.

Being an online campaign or email builder, it is also mobile. So you can work on your campaigns from your laptop at home, in a coffee shop and even on your phone.

Excellent analytics.

It is exciting to see how well your campaign or mail is doing. How many people opened the mail, how many people clicked your links and even how many of your customers forwarded it to another friend. This can also help you with sales analytics that will show you where sales come from. It will also show you which of your links are clicked most. Is it the links at the bottom or the links at the top of the email? Is it perhaps a specific image that you included in your mail that grabbed the attention. This you can then again use to have more successful campaigns via Facebook and Instagram ads.

It also allows for A/B testing. A/B testing is creating two mails with similar content (maybe different text, images, headlines, videos), marketing the same products. It gets sent to two test groups to see which mail gets the most engagement. Then when you have decided which campaign you are going to use, it mails that one (the one with most engagement) to your customers.

Organic and manual growing.

Organic growing is when customers sign up to your mailing list themselves. This could be from a Facebook post or from an email that was forwarded to them from a friend.

It also has admin functionality that allows you to manually add customers to the list. You might have collected a few email addresses offline which you can manually add. If it is a long list of contact details, it also has the functionality to import the entire address list and will update already existing contacts should the email address already exist in your mailing list.

E-commerce integrations.

Mailing list software also usually have native integrations to some of the software you might be using, like Shopify or Clickfunnels. Jumping quickly back to analytics (as discussed), it will match up sales that originated from people clicking on the mail to sales in your online store. So in your metrics, it will give you an idea of how many sales originated from your mail campaign.

Accessing on the go.

We have already touched on this briefly. Just like productivity tools, you want to see and even manage things while you are out or about. Because your mailing list software is online, you can access it from virtually everywhere, your phone, a friend's phone or computer, even an internet cafe.

Mailing software that I use:

Mailchimp

Sign-up: https://bit.ly/3awK4Q5
Sign-up is free but there is an option to move to the paid-for service once you have 2000 people in your mailing list or you want to start scheduling campaigns, do A/B testing and multistep journeys.

12 SHIPPING

What is shipping and why do I need it?

So far we have dealt a lot on the moving parts that need to be in place to provide your customer with a great shipping experience. And we know what is required to be in place to start marketing your business and products. Once your customers have placed their orders, you will be required to get them the goods (or services) they have ordered. Commerce is an exchange, they exchange money for goods and services. Shipping might not be as integral to provide a specific service, but it is vital to get customers their goods.

Shipping needs to be handled carefully as it could become a major expense to your business. It might also be that low-cost items might attract a similar shipping cost to a more expensive item. Your customer might not think twice about adding R100 courier to an R1,000 item. But when he purchased an R80 item, an additional R100 for shipping might be a dealbreaker.

Strategy 101.
There are things customers like and things they don't like. Normally shipping is one of the things they do not like. They'll spend R200 on fuel to drive an pick up an item, but they think twice when they have to pay R100 to have it shipped. But all is not in vain. There are easy ways to give customers a free shipping offer (and Shopify allows you to do them all).

The first strategy:
For high ticket items, try and provide free shipping. Even if your product is R50 more expensive than in Joe Soaps shop, if Joe charges R100 shipping and

you manage to absorb the shipping cost in your price and advertise the item as free shipping, chances are very good that the customer will likely conclude the sale at your store. Strange but true. Therefore when offering products, try to absorb as much of the shipping in the cost so that you can either provide free shipping or low shipping fees.

The second strategy:

Purchasing products or a combination that exceed a certain rand value, qualifies for free shipping. There is a well established online shop in South Africa that uses this strategy very successfully. Once your order is over a certain amount, for example, R450, the customer qualifies for free shipping. This is very useful to inspire the customer to purchase more items from your shop. If their shopping cart value for example purposes are R400, they need to pay the R100 courier fee, but should they purchase an additional item that would push them over the R450 threshold, then they get free shipping.

The third strategy:

Give your customer the option to collect from you for free. This comes back to the psychology that they would rather spend R200 on fuel than R100 on courier costs. If at all possible, offer this service as it results in zero packaging costs to you, so there is already a little save. Also, I have found that some customers do not mind to courier, but on their first order, they choose the collect option just to see where I operate from and meet me in person. People like to know who they are dealing with.

The fourth strategy:

If all else fails and you have to charge courier, charge a single courier cost (try and keep it the same for everyone). This would probably take some trial and error. What I have found in my business and shipping products is that some parcels only costs R65 to courier and others R130 to courier, so I charge a flat rate of R100. Because I will score on the R65 shipments and that would balance out the R130 shipments.

Packaging.

As you would potentially ship more orders than gets collected, ensure that your products are properly packaged for shipping to protect the contents. Make sure you have the basic supplies:

- Bubble wrap
- Shipping boxes
- Boxing tape

- Scissors
- Fragile stickers
- Pen
- Printer (for Waybills)

Your packaging can be used to distinguish you from your competitors but can quickly become very expensive. Branded boxes are a great way to do this and to market your product, as it would potentially be seen by friends and family who are there when the products get delivered. But they could be expensive. An alternative to this is making use of inserts. It could be a small handwritten thank you note on printed stationery. Maybe a business card or even a bumper sticker.

The most important thing regarding packaging is, that it should be lightweight because in the end the product that ships consist of the weight of the product plus the weight of the shipping. The heavier the parcel, the more you might end up paying to ship.

Insurance and Tracking.

Using a form of shipping, like a courier, can go a long way in giving your customers peace of mind. Once you book in the parcel with your courier you will be issued with a tracking number. It is a great way to inform your customer that his/her parcel is on its way. When using a shopfront like Shopify, you can add tracking details as soon as you fulfil their order. This will kick off a mail to your customer informing them that their parcel has shipped. If your shopfront does not provide this functionality, using a messenger service or email will put your customer's mind at ease that what he paid for is on its way and that he can track the parcel to see when it will arrive.

Providing insurance on a parcel is another way to set your customer's mind at ease, especially if it is a high-value item. That way, should something happen to the parcel in transit, you and the customer will be covered. Some courier services already have insurance built it, others don't, so be sure to check with the courier what service they provide in terms of insurance and what the costs would be.

Labelling packages.

Ensure that parcels and waybills are legible. Therefore it is a good idea to get a printer to print your courier waybills rather than witing them by hand. You don't want the courier, when out delivering the parcel, not being able to read a contact number or deliver the parcel to an incorrect address. There are always lots of different printers on the market that does this just fine. Printing in colour looks very professional but it comes at a price. If you don't already own a printer, try to get a monochrome (black and white) inkjet printer for starters. They are usually quite affordable but have a slightly higher running cost in printer cartridges. Once you are more established, look at obtaining a laser printer with scanning capabilities. Their initial cost is usually much higher than inkjets, but in the long run, it will save you money in toner as opposed to inkjet cartridges.

Shipping will form a fundamental part of of your e-commerce business.
Shipping does come with a few challenges, but as you start shipping out more parcels, you will quickly discover what works and what to tweak. Within a few months, you will have developed an efficient shipping strategy.

Understanding all the variables and evolving your shipping strategy with your growing business is vital to long term business success. Once you have figured it out, don't shy away from reevaluating your shipping strategy to deliver the absolute best customer experience.

Shipping and courier companies I use:

The Courier Guy

Sign-up: https://bit.ly/2Lotppu
Sign-up requires a R 1,150 deposit for opening the Pre-Paid account (which is what I use). As this is a pre-paid account, your account will be credited with your R 1,150 deposit which shipping costs will get deducted from as you start shipping.

PostNet
With PostNet, you will most likely have to go into a PostNet near you and the friendly staff will assist you in shipping your packages to a PostNet close to your customer. PostNet has a very wide network of pickup and dropoff points and you will find that some customers prefer them. They are especially useful for customers living on farms, who will get notified once the parcel reached their PostNet and when the parcel is ready for collection. I have also found that the Aramex app is very useful in tracking parcels you send using PostNet.

12 IN CLOSING

This is the first book in the series about starting an online business in South Africa. There are obviously many ways to go about starting an online business. There are also other online presence and social tools that can help you along your journey. In South Africa, we have quite a few banks and different account you can choose from and also numerous payment processors you can use.

This book is primarily written from my point of view and everything I had to figure out to start my online business. The tools and technologies mentioned in the book are the ones I am familiar with. Because of this, it is also the tools and services I am in the best position to advise on as I am actively using them.

In the next book, we will look at analytics and the marketing strategies I used to get my business going. We will cover organic strategies (which is time-consuming but will get you off the ground with minimal spend) as well as paid strategies. A new business can definitely grow organically (minimal financial spend) through the tactics I will discuss. This will enable you to delay ad-spend in the beginning until such time as you reach the ceiling, just like I did. At that point, going to a paid-for ad strategy will have you continue to see growth in your business.

ABOUT THE AUTHOR

Johan Renier Gertzen holds a Bachelor of Commerce in Informatics, majoring in Informatics as well as Industrial Psychology. He has worked actively in the Information Technology sector for over 20 years. During his career, he has attained a wealth of knowledge and experience in several IT disciplines, including website design, website hosting and e-commerce. He lives with his wife and children in Johannesburg, South Africa.

www.ingramcontent.com/pod-product-compliance
Lightning Source LLC
Chambersburg PA
CBHW071049220526
45467CB00004B/1739